What does God's Word say about anger?

by Afia Keteku

What does God's Word say about anger?

Published by ETAK Publishing Services

Cover Design by Afia Keteku

For adults

The book is recommended for children between the ages of 5 and 11.

There are certain words and phrases that may need to be explained to children.

A glossary has been provided at the back of the book to explain some of the words that children may find difficult to understand. Children may also use a dictionary to find out more about certain words.

Questions are provided at the end of the book for children to check their understanding.

The text is short and direct and points children to the important difference between godly anger and human anger. It helps children to understand why godly anger is useful and how human anger can be destructive and unhelpful.

If your child is interested in finding out more Bible verses about anger, some have been provided at the end of the book.

Acknowledgements

Thanks to my amazing husband, Evame, for supporting and encouraging me. You are simply the best!

And special thanks to my pastor, Chris Gill, for reviewing the manuscript and providing some invaluable insights.

Dedications

Dedicated to my children, Mawulikem and Mawulorm, who give me more to write about than I could ever imagine. I love you to bits.

What is anger?

Anger is a strong feeling you get when you are annoyed with something or someone.

Anger is one of the emotions God gave us when He created us and there was a very good reason for it.

When God made man, He gave man the power to rule over the earth. If things were not going as God had planned, man would get very uncomfortable and angry. That God-given anger would give man the energy he needed to correct the things that were going wrong.

When man disobeyed God, he lost his true identity and became selfish and wicked. Instead of getting angry at the things that made God unhappy, man got angry at the things that made ***him*** unhappy.

The godly anger God had created to be a good thing was destroyed. It was now human anger and it was very destructive.

A closer look at godly anger

God gets angry!

When people do not respect God and His laws, and instead make other things more important than God, it hurts God and makes Him angry.

Let's look at some examples of God's anger in the Bible.

We read in 1 Kings chapter 11 verse 9,

'So the LORD became angry with Solomon, because his heart had turned from the LORD God of Israel….' (NKJV)

Isaiah chapter 42 verses 24b to 25a says,

'For they would not follow his ways; they did not obey his law.
So he poured out on them his burning anger...' (NIV)

Romans chapter 1 verses 18 and 21,

'God's anger is revealed from heaven against all the sin and evil of the people whose evil ways prevent the truth from being known....... They know God, but they do not give him the honour that belongs to him..' (GNT)

From these verses, we see that the reason God was angry was because people did not love and obey Him.

The example of Jesus

Jesus went into the temple one day and found people selling doves, changing up money and treating the house of God like a marketplace!

Jesus got really angry!

He overturned the tables of the money-changers. He got a whip and drove out those selling birds.

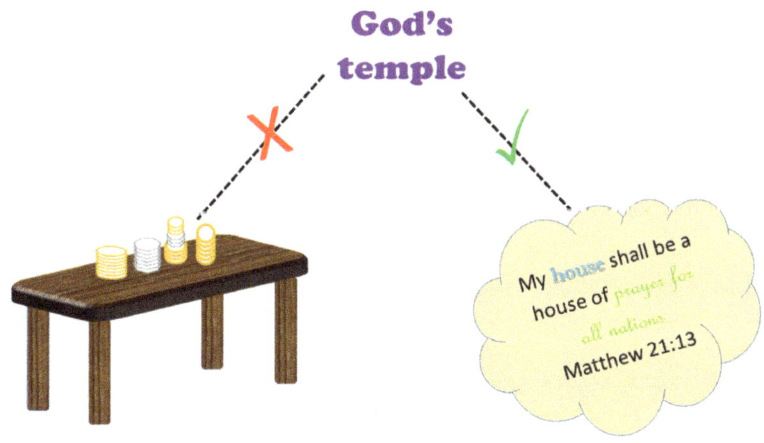

Why was Jesus so annoyed?

In Matthew 21 verse 13 we read,
'And He said to them, "It is written, 'My house shall be called a house of prayer,' but you have made it a 'den of thieves.' "' (NKJV)

God never wanted the temple to be used for selling. He wanted it to be a place where people would come to worship and pray to Him. The temple was to be a holy and sacred place.

By selling in the temple, the sellers had disobeyed God's command. They were offering sacrifices in the temple but their hearts were no longer obedient to God.

God's love for us

God hates sin, and He gets angry when there is sin and disobedience.

But God also loves us deeply and provides a way for us to be free from the power of sin.

John chapter 3 verses 16 and 36 tell us,

‘For God so loved the world that he gave his one and only Son, that whoever believes in him shall not perish but have eternal life.........Whoever believes in the Son has eternal life, but whoever rejects the Son will not see life, for God’s wrath remains on them.’ (NIV)

God loves us so much that He gave us Jesus.

When we believe in Jesus, our sins are forgiven. Jesus died to pay the price for our sins so that God will not be angry with us anymore.

God is angry with evil

When someone is evil, they do bad things. They hurt themselves and others and, most of all, make God sad.

Psalm 7 verse 11 tells us,

‘God is a righteous judge, a God who is angry at evil every single day.’ (CEB)

God is righteous which means that He is perfect and holy. It also means that He cannot stand sin.

God gets angry with evil because evil separates us from God.

God is slow to anger

Even though God is very angry when He is not obeyed and His laws are broken, God shows us great mercy and gives us an opportunity to realise the bad choices we have made.

God's anger is mixed with so much sadness because he knows the wrong choices we have made will harm us. His heart grieves that we have turned our backs on His ways.

Psalm 103:8 tells us,

'The Lord is merciful and gracious, slow to anger, and abounding in mercy.' (NKJV)

Did you know that in the Hebrew language, the word for *slow* is 'long' and the word for *anger* is 'nose'? That means when it comes to anger, God is described as having a 'long nose'! In other words, He doesn't break out in anger as soon as we sin (short nose); instead He controls his anger and gives us time to repent and come back to Him for forgiveness.

Human anger and God's righteousness

Now that we've looked at the anger of God, and why He gets angry, let's look at human anger.

James 1:19-20 says,

'....... Everyone should be quick to listen, slow to speak and slow to become angry because human anger does not produce the righteousness God desires' (NIV)

The passage makes it clear that we should be slow in getting angry.

Getting angry quickly does not allow us to assess the situation and act wisely. A person who is easily and quickly angered is more likely to do foolish things, cause more trouble and get themselves into a lot of trouble.

Human anger is hardly ever slow. It is easily provoked, it is unrestrained, it is not motivated by love and it is not mixed with mercy.

Most importantly, human anger does not result in people coming back into a right relationship with God. It does not lead to the righteousness God originally wanted anger to produce.

Human anger is destructive

Human anger is ungodly. Instead of producing healing and righteousness, it leads to damage and makes a bad situation worse.

When people have ungodly anger, they usually get into a very violent mood. They kick things, stamp their feet, say unkind words, spoil things and most of all, hurt people.

Being angry and destructive is like driving a nail into a plank of wood.

You can pull the nail out of the wood but you may never be able to completely fix the hole in the wood.

The story of Cain

Cain and his brother Abel brought offerings to God. Abel brought the right offering but Cain did not. God rejected Cain's offering but He was really pleased with Abel's.

Cain should have been sorry that he did not bring the right offering. He should have asked God to forgive him and help him do the right thing.

Instead, Cain got extremely jealous of his brother. 'Why was Abel's offering accepted and mine wasn't? That is not fair', thought Cain.

The more evil he thought about, the angrier he became.

God said to Cain,

'Why are you angry?.....if you do not do well, sin lies at your door. And its desire is for you….' (Genesis 4:6 – 7) (NKJV)

God wanted Cain to stop being so angry and mend his ways, but Cain did not listen to God.

In fact, Cain continued being so angry that he killed his brother Abel!

Human anger leads to fighting

The Bible says a lot about how ungodly anger makes us think and behave.

Proverbs chapter 29 verse 22 says,

'People with quick tempers cause a lot of quarrelling and trouble.' (GNT)

Being quick-tempered means getting angry very quickly. Being quick-tempered causes lots of arguments and misunderstanding. When quick-tempered people are around, the atmosphere is always volatile. Fights break out very quickly and there's no peace.

Proverbs chapter 15 verse 18 also tells us,

‘A hot-tempered person stirs up conflict, but the one who is patient calms a quarrel.’ (NIV)

Nobody wants to be around someone who is always creating serious disagreements. Everybody wants to be around a person with a calm attitude who creates an atmosphere of peace and calm.

Do you want to be an angry person or a calm person?

Human anger is foolish

The Bible uses a very strong word to describe people with quick tempers. Look at the verses below:

Proverbs chapter 14 verse 29,

‘Whoever is patient has great understanding, but one who is quick-tempered displays **folly**.’ (NIV)

Ecclesiastes 7:9,

‘Do not be quickly provoked in your spirit, for anger resides in the lap of **fools**.’

Proverbs 29:11,

‘**Fools** give full vent to their rage, but the wise bring calm in the end.’

All the bold words in the verses point to one root word — ‘fool’.

The Bible calls angry and hot-tempered people fools! Ouch!

You wouldn't want to be described as a fool, would you?

Being friends with angry people

Now let's look at what the Bible says about being friends with angry people.

In Proverbs chapter 22 verse 24, we read,

'Do not make friends with a hot-tempered person, do not associate with one easily angered' (NIV)

The Bible advises people not to be friends with you if you are quick-tempered and angry.

It is sad not to have friends, isn't it?

Dealing with human anger

The Bible provides help on how to deal with human and ungodly anger.

First of all, you need to ask Jesus to help you use anger in the way God intended. God wants you to be angry at the thing that makes Him angry: sin.

But He also wants that anger to be tinged with the same mercy and love He shows us when we sin.

You can ask him to come and help you by praying this simple prayer:

'Lord Jesus, I need you in my life. You died to pay the price so that I can be free. I thank you for dying for me. Lord, please come into my heart. Forgive me for all the bad things I have said and done. Help me to realise the power you give me to overcome all sin, including ungodly anger. Thank you, Father God, that I am now your child. In Jesus' name I pray, Amen.'

A new creation

The Bible says in 2 Corinthians chapter 5 verse 17,

'Therefore, if anyone is in Christ, he is a new creation; old things have passed away; behold, all things have become new.' (NKJV)

Being in Christ simply means that you have become part of Him. You do not own yourself anymore; you belong to Christ.

When you get a new folder in school, the teacher writes your name on the folder. Everyone who picks up that folder knows it is yours because they notice your name on it.

In the same way, anyone who looks at you now knows you belong to Jesus because He 'writes' his name on you.

You are HIS!

Colossians chapter 3 verse 1 says,

'Since then you have been raised with Christ, set your minds on things above…' (NIV)

Then in Colossians chapter 3 verse 8, we are told,

'... you must also rid yourselves of all such things as these: anger, rage, malice, slander, and filthy language from your lips' (NIV)

Now that we have asked Jesus to take over our lives and we are His, we must remove bad things from our lives.

Human anger is one of those bad things. Remember, you are in Christ — you have a new identity and a new name.

In your anger, do not sin

Now, for some very helpful verses.

Ephesians chapter 4 verses 26 and 27 tell us,

'In your anger, do not sin; do not let the sun go down while you are still angry. And give no place to the devil.' (NIV)

Let's look at these verses bit by bit.

'In your anger, do not sin..'

The anger in this passage refers to godly anger. We are told in this verse to make sure that while we are expressing godly anger over wrongdoing, we **do not sin**.

This is because anger, even godly anger, is a very, very strong emotion. The energy anger gives us takes over the way we think, talk and react. We need to be careful that we use that energy in the right way — to correct with love; not to destroy.

The only way to use godly anger properly is to ask Jesus to help us do the right thing.

As we rely on the Holy Spirit of God, we will be able to direct our anger at the things that make God mad.

'..do not let the sun go down when you are still angry..'

Do not let your godly anger go on for longer than necessary. Do not let the thing you are righteously angry about go uncorrected. Take prompt action to correct the wrong in the way the Holy Spirit leads you to. Then let go of the anger.

'And give no place to the devil'

When a friend visits you, you make the friend feel welcome. You may take them to your garden to play with them, get them a drink or share your toys with them. You give them 'place' in your house — you make them happy so that they want to come back and visit.

Even when we feel godly anger at evil, we need to make sure that we align our energy with God's Word.

If we don't, we make the devil feel welcome. We give him 'place' — which makes him extremely happy because he can always come back and visit!

I'm sure you don't want the devil to be your friend, do you?

Slowly count to 10!

The next time you feel yourself getting angry,

S-l-o-w-l-y COUNT TO 10.

This will give you time to assess your anger and ask yourself some really important questions:

1. Am I angry at something that would make God angry?

2. Am I angry because God's word is being disobeyed?

3. Am I sad because God's laws are being broken?

4. Will my thoughts to correct the bad situation make God happy?

5. Will my actions make the situation better and not worse?

If while you are angry, you are thinking of doing or saying something harmful, beware and STOP!
Ask God to flood your heart with His Spirit so that you don't do anything stupid.

Remember, human anger does not result in the righteousness God wants.

Let your anger be godly and use it to correct sin and wrongdoing; not to destroy things or people.

Galatians 5 verses 16 and 22 to 23a tell us:

'I say then: Walk in the Spirit, and you shall not fulfil the lust of the flesh.......the fruit of the Spirit is love, joy, peace, longsuffering, kindness, goodness, faithfulness, gentleness, **self-control**.' (NKJV)

As you rely on the Holy Spirit every single day, He will give you the strength and desire to control yourself and only get angry about the things that make God angry.

Can you remember what makes

angry

Glossary

Identity – who a person is or what a thing is

Provoke – if you provoke someone, you typically make them angry

Sacred – another word for holy

Unrestrained – something or someone that cannot be stopped

Violent – a very strong force which can often be dangerous

Volatile – something which is likely to change very quickly and without warning; that change could lead to something bad

Bible translations used

CEB – Common English Bible

GNT – Good News Translation

NIV – New International Version

NKJV – New King James Version

Questions

What is anger?

Why did God create anger?

What happened to anger when man disobeyed God?

Why does God get angry?

What can we do to avoid God's anger?

What is the difference between godly anger and human anger?

In your own words, describe human anger.

What is one thing you can do the next time you get angry?

Other Bible verses about anger

Proverbs 15:1

Proverbs 19:11

Proverbs 29:11

Psalm 37: 8-9

Proverbs 14:17

Proverbs 17:27

James 4:1-2

Matthew 5:22

About the author

Afia lives in Kent with her husband and two kids.

In her spare time, she enjoys writing, singing and sewing.

She also loves working with children and teaches in the children's service in her church.

Her passion is to see children love God and understand His plans for their lives.

www.ingramcontent.com/pod-product-compliance
Ingram Content Group UK Ltd.
Pitfield, Milton Keynes, MK11 3LW, UK
UKHW062300290726
14090UKWH00017B/802

9 781518 446795